First Word Book

KINGFISHER

KINGFISHER
Kingfisher Publications Plc
New Penderel House
283-288 High Holborn
London WC1V 7HZ

First published by Kingfisher Publications Plc 2000
2 4 6 8 10 9 7 5 3 1

1TR/0701/TIMS/MAR(MAR)/128MA

A CIP catalogue record of this book is available from the British Library.

ISBN 0 7534 0645 4

Printed in China

Editor: Camilla Reid
Senior Designer: Sarah Goodwin
Illustrator: Mandy Stanley
DTP Co-ordinator: Nicky Studdart
Production: Caroline Jackson
Educational Consultant: Jeni Riley

Contents

Suggestions for parents

Sharing a favourite book with your child is the ideal way of helping him or her learn to read. This colourful, appealing first word book will act as an invaluable prompt for looking at, discussing and labelling everyday objects, and it will establish the skills needed for confident reading.

Very young children will enjoy browsing through the book, pointing out objects they recognise. Encourage them to show you what they know about each picture and give them plenty of praise, even if they get things wrong. For toddlers, the book will help them to learn about both spoken words and written words and the connections between the two. This is important in the very earliest stages of learning to read.

When reading this book with your child, we suggest you progress through the steps listed opposite. Try to create a relaxed, non-pressurized atmosphere and allow your child to work at his or her own pace. Above all, remember that for learning to be valuable, it should also be fun!

4

1. Point to the objects on each page. Say each label then ask the child to repeat them. After several readings, he or she will start to say the names unprompted.

2. Match the spoken word to the written label next to the picture. Encourage your child to run a finger along the written label (this develops the understanding that a spoken word has a written equivalent).

3. Select a picture label and ask your child to find the same word in the list that runs along the bottom of the page. This teaches the child to recognise the shape of the word, an essential pre-reading skill. Initially, the child may just realise that the text looks the same, but eventually you can point out the shape and distinctive features of the individual letters.

4. Encourage your child to identify words by the common initial sound/letter, and then to realise that a letter (or group of letters) represents a sound within a word, e.g. the ch of chick.

Enjoy your reading!

Jeni Riley

Jeni Riley M.A., Ph.D., Head of Primary Education,
Institute of Education, University of London

What's in the bedroom?

6

ball

teddy bear

pen

pencil

lamp   pen   bed   comb   doll   yo-yo

bed

lamp

yo-yo

rug

comb

kite

book

doll

kite   ball   pencil   rug   book   teddy bear

Things we see in the kitchen

fork

knife

spoon

iron

plate

bowl

spoon   mop   bib   jar   mat   pan

jar

pan

mop

bib

mat

cup

cup   fork   bowl   iron   plate   knife

It's bathtime!

bath

duck

sponge

towel

toothbrush sink potty door bath soap

sink

door

mirror

potty

toothpaste

soap

toothbrush

toothpaste   mirror   duck   towel   sponge

Getting dressed

T-shirt

skirt

jeans

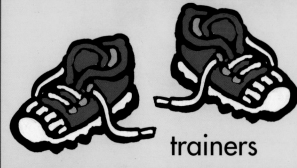

trainers

socks

jumper   shoes   cap   T-shirt   skirt   gloves

coat

gloves

jumper

shoes

belt

cap

scarf

trainers   scarf   belt   jeans   socks   coat

13

Point to these parts of your body

nose

toe

back

chin

ear   back   nose   hand   knee   foot

ear

hair

foot

hand

arm

eye

leg

knee

hair   eye   arm   leg   chin   toe

What food do you like to eat?

pineapple

bread

banana

orange

egg

pie

lolly   strawberry   carrot   bread   cheese   pie

ham

carrot

cheese

apple

strawberry

lolly

banana   pineapple   egg   orange   ham   apple

Look around the garden

butterfly

slug

rake

ant

ladybird

worm   cobweb   frog   ant   gate   butterfly

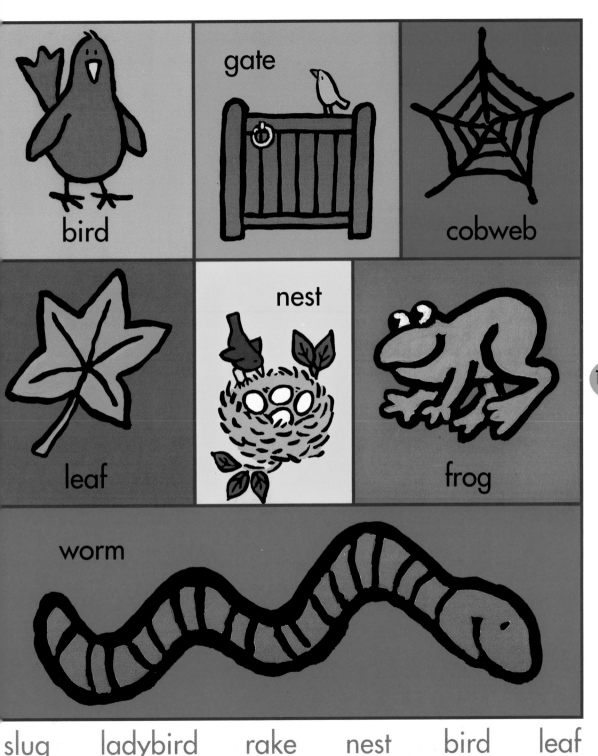

bird

gate

cobweb

leaf

nest

frog

worm

slug ladybird rake nest bird leaf

Let's go to the park!

pushchair

sandpit

dog

pond

flower   tricycle   rollerblades   see-saw   pond

flower

swing

rollerblades

tricycle

tree

slide

see-saw

swing   tree   sandpit   dog   pushchair   slide

There's lots to do at school

table

teacher

paints

paintbrush

bricks   rucksack   blackboard   chair   table

drawers

bricks

scissors

rucksack

chair

blackboard

paints   scissors   paintbrush   teacher   drawers

The supermarket is a busy place

milk

jam

trolley

assistant

box   purse   tin   juice   till   vegetables

vegetables

bag

box

tin

25

juice

purse

money

money   bag   assistant   milk   trolley   jam

We are going to a party

cake

candle

balloon

present

sandwich

party-blower

bow   candle   sweets   hat   present   straw

jelly

bow

sweets

hat

straw

cake   balloon   sandwich   party-blower   jelly

Who are these people?

man

woman

girl

boy

baby

girl   clown   nurse   boy   dancer   spy

vet

chef

dancer

clown

spy

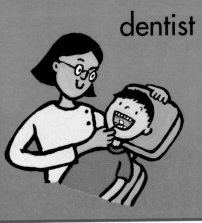

dentist

nurse

chef   baby   dentist   man   vet   woman

Things that go

ship

rocket

car

aeroplane

bus

motorbike   train   bicycle   rocket   lorry   car

bicycle

boat

hot-air balloon

lorry

motorbike

train

boat   ship   hot-air balloon   bus   aeroplane

Come for a day on the farm!

tractor

goat

barn

pig

bull

cat   sheep   house   farmer   chick   bull

house

chick

farmer

calf

sheep

cow

cat

goat   calf   pig   barn   cow   tractor

Where do these animals live?

tiger

wolf

swan

deer

bear parrot deer tiger seal monkey

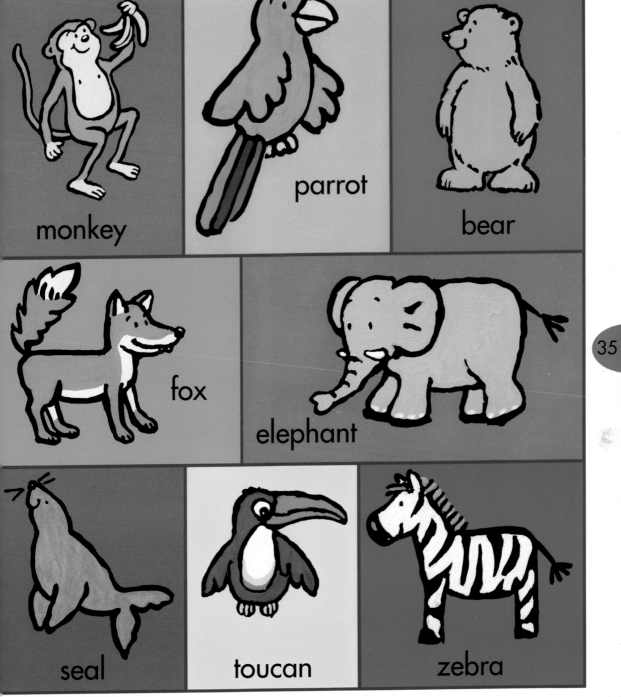

monkey

parrot

bear

fox

elephant

seal

toucan

zebra

zebra   fox   elephant   wolf   swan   toucan

Having fun at the seaside

starfish

sea

flip-flops

fish

yacht

sea   bucket   crab   shell   fish   sandcastle

eel

sandcastle

crab

spade

net

bucket

shell

net   spade   yacht   flip-flops   eel   starfish

What's the weather like?

sun

hail

lightning

fog

rain

storm   wind   ice   hail   cloud   sun

ice

snow

moon

cloud

wind

storm

rain   moon   lightning   snow   fog

What sounds do these make?

bang bang

drum

horse

clip clop

bee

buzz buzz

ding dong

bell

woof woof

dog

mouse snake lamb bee trumpet lion

telephone

ring ring

snake

hiss hiss

squeak squeak

mouse

baa baa

lamb

lion

roar roar

toot toot

trumpet

owl

twit twoo

bell   owl   horse   drum   telephone   dog

Can you name these shapes?

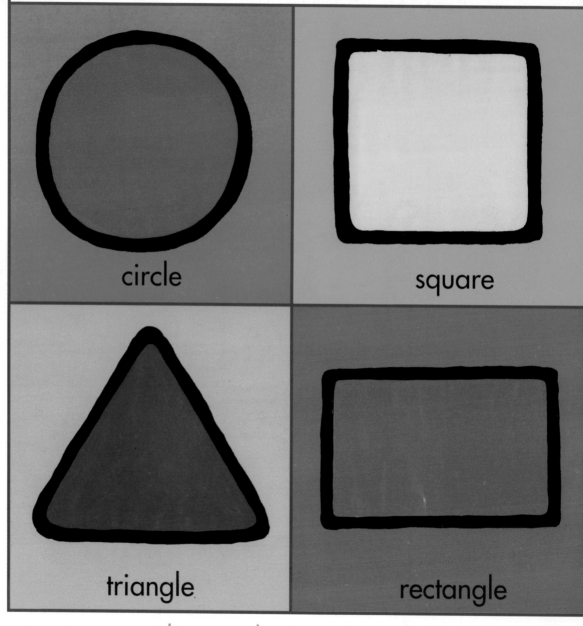

circle

square

triangle

rectangle

square   diamond   star   rectangle

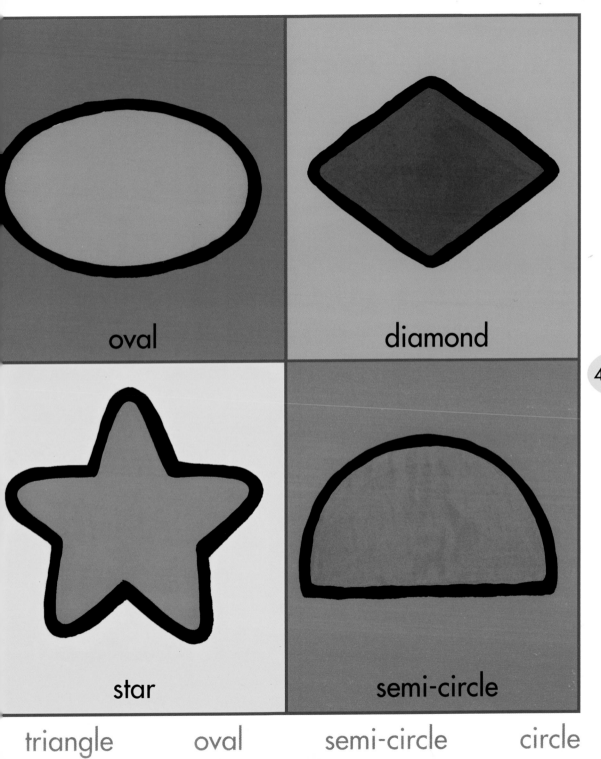

oval

diamond

star

semi-circle

triangle   oval   semi-circle   circle

All sorts of opposites

fat

thin

old

young

slow

fast

big   young   up   short   fast   thin

up

down

tall

short

big

small

slow   small   tall   down   old   fat

What's your favourite colour?

black

yellow

blue

green

white   brown   pink   yellow   orange

grey

purple

red

brown

pink

white

orange

47

grey   black   green   purple   red   blue

Word list

A
aeroplane	30
ant	18
apple	17
arm	15
assistant	24

B
baby	28
back	14
bag	25
ball	6
balloon	26
banana	16
barn	32
bath	10
bear	35
bed	7
bee	40
bell	40
belt	13
bib	9
bicycle	31
big	45
bird	19
black	46
blackboard	23
blue	46
boat	31
book	7
bow	27
bowl	8
box	25
boy	28
bread	16
bricks	23
brown	47
bucket	37
bull	32
bus	30
butterfly	18

C
cake	26
calf	33
candle	26
cap	13
car	30
carrot	17
cat	33
chair	23
cheese	17
chef	29
chick	33
chin	14
circle	42
cloud	39

clown	29
coat	13
cobweb	19
comb	7
cow	33
crab	37
cup	9

D
dancer	29
deer	34
dentist	29
diamond	43
dog	20, 40
doll	7
door	11
down	45
drawers	23
drum	40
duck	10

E
ear	15
eel	37
egg	16
elephant	35
eye	15

F
farmer	33
fast	44
fat	44
fish	36
flip-flops	36
flower	21
fog	38
foot	15
fork	8
fox	35
frog	19

G
gate	19
girl	28
gloves	13
goat	32
green	46
grey	47

H
hail	38
hair	15
ham	17
hand	15
hat	27
horse	40
hot-air balloon	31

house	33

I
ice	39
iron	8

J
jam	24
jar	9
jeans	12
jelly	27
juice	25
jumper	13

K
kite	7
knee	15
knife	8

L
ladybird	18
lamb	41
lamp	7
leaf	19
leg	15
lightning	38
lion	41
lolly	17
lorry	31

M
man	28
mat	9
milk	24
mirror	11
money	25
monkey	35
moon	39
mop	9
motorbike	31
mouse	41

N
nest	19
net	37
nose	14
nurse	29

O
old	44
orange	16, 47
oval	43
owl	41

P
paintbrush	22
paints	22

pan	9
parrot	35
party-blower	26
pen	6
pencil	6
pie	16
pig	32
pineapple	16
pink	47
plate	8
pond	20
potty	11
present	26
purple	47
purse	25
pushchair	20

R
rain	38
rake	18
rectangle	42
red	47
rocket	30
rollerblades	21
rucksack	23
rug	7

S
sandcastle	37
sandpit	20
sandwich	26
scarf	13
scissors	23
sea	36
seal	35
see-saw	21
semi-circle	43
sheep	33
shell	37
ship	30
shoes	13
short	45
sink	11
skirt	12
slide	21
slow	44
slug	18
small	45
snake	41
snow	39
soap	11
socks	12
spade	37
sponge	10
spoon	8
spy	29
square	42

star	43
starfish	36
storm	39
straw	27
strawberry	17
sun	38
swan	34
sweets	27
swing	21

T
table	22
tall	45
teacher	22
teddy bear	6
telephone	41
thin	44
tiger	34
till	25
tin	25
toe	14
toothbrush	11
toothpaste	11
toucan	35
towel	10
tractor	32
train	31
trainers	12
tree	21
triangle	42
tricycle	21
trolley	24
trumpet	41
T-shirt	12

U
up	45

V
vegetables	25
vet	29

W
white	47
wind	39
wolf	34
woman	28
worm	19

Y
yacht	36
yellow	46
young	44
yo-yo	7

Z
zebra	35